Causes and Campaigns

Jenny Vaughan

amicus

Published by Amicus
P.O. Box 1329, Mankato, Minnesota 56002

Printed in the United States of America at Corporate Graphics, in North Mankato, Minnesota.

Published by arrangement with the Watts Publishing Group Ltd., London.

Library of Congress Cataloging-in-Publication Data

Vaughan, Jenny, 1947-
   Causes and campaigns / by Jenny Vaughan.
      p. cm. -- (Media power)
   Summary: "Discusses the media treatment of social campaigns worldwide, including media coverage of causes such as natural disasters, AIDS, global warming, and how the media can affect these
campaigns"--Provided by publisher.
   Includes index.
   ISBN 978-1-60753-111-1 (library binding)
   1. Communication in social action--Juvenile literature. 2. Mass media--Social
aspects--Juvenile literature. 3. Mass media--Influence--Juvenile literature. 4. Mass media--Audi-
ences--Juvenile literature. 5. Public relations--Juvenile literature. I. Title.
   HN90.M3V38 2011
   659.2'93244--dc22

                                                                          2009041832

Series editor: Julia Bird
Design: Nimbus Design

Picture credits:
Action Press/Rex Features: 13; Advertising Archives: 11, 26, 33; J. Scott Applewhite/AP/PA Photos: 40; Adrian Arbib/Corbis: 21;
Bettmann/Corbis: 18; Hubert Boesl/DPA/PA Photos: 15; Manuel Citak/Greenpeace: 31; Emmanuel Dunnard/epa/Corbis: 17; Du-
rand-Hudson-Langevin-Orbon/Sygma/Corbis: 39; Tod A Gipstein/Corbis: 34; Louise Gubb/SABA/Corbis: 27. Fiona Hanson/PA
Photos: 30; Jeremy Horner/Corbis: 19; Steven Kazlowski/Ecoscene: 38. Owaki Kulia/Corbis: 22; Christopher Morris/Corbis: 36;
Claudio Onorati/epa/Corbis: 41. Thierry Orban/Corbis: 23; Warwick Page/Corbis: 12; Photos 12/Alamy: 25; Brian Branch
Price/AP.PA Photos: 28; Pulse PL/PA Photos: 29; Chris Radburn/PA Archive/PA Photos: 8. Reuters/Corbis: 20, 35; Rex Features:
24; Julian Simmonds/Rex Features: 32; Slpa Press/Rex Features: 9, 14; Steve Starr/Corbis: 10; David Turnley/Corbis: 37; Aubrey
Wade/Panos: 16.

With thanks to Barry White at the Campaign for Press
and Broadcasting Freedom for help and advice (http://www.cpbf.org.uk)

1212
32010   8915

9 8 7 6 5 4 3 2 1

Contents

Campaigning and the Media

Campaigns are activities that support or draw attention to a particular cause. All campaigns need people behind them, whether they donate money directly to the cause or help do the work of the campaign. The best way to get supporters is to use the media to communicate with the world about the cause behind the campaign.

Which Media?

The media includes magazines, newspapers, television and radio (known as broadcasting), the Internet and e-mail, books, plays, and films. Campaigns that involve national or international issues, such as combating world poverty, need to use media that will reach as many people as possible. These campaigns try to get national newspapers, radio, and television stations interested in their causes by writing to them, calling them, or sending them press releases.

Campaigns around much smaller, local issues—such as keeping a school or library open or making a section of road safer—use locally based newspapers, radio stations, and television stations.

A local campaign, such as this one against a new road bypass, needs the support of local papers and radio to attract people's attention.

Blogging On

Campaigners can use the Internet to let people know about their cause. Many send out regular e-mails to supporters or produce online news and blogs. Some groups make their own films for television, which they can also post on their web sites.

Media coverage of humanitarian crises, such as the civil war in the Darfur region of Sudan, encourages the public to give money to help refugees and puts political pressure on governments and aid agencies.

The Media at Work

Good journalists will do their best to find out as much about a campaign as possible—and may end up showing that campaigners are wrong about an issue or are conducting a campaign poorly. Both positive and negative media coverage play a vital role in informing people about a campaign or cause.

• Up for Discussion •

How can campaigners choose the right media to give publicity to their cause?

Is it possible to run a campaign without involving the media? How?

Money Talks

Public Relations (PR) is the business of getting a point of view across to the public, usually through the media. Wealthy campaigners can spend large sums on PR. The result can sometimes be a one-sided, or even misleading, account of the facts.

The High Cost of Campaigning Media

There are specialty PR companies that campaign in various ways, such as conducting surveys, organizing conferences, publishing research, and employing experts—all to get the right information to the media. Good PR can help campaigners to lobby (try to influence) governments. It helps if they can show that they have public support.

Campaign Giants

One example is the oil giant Exxon. It funded groups that campaigned to question the science of climate change —the view among scientists that burning fossil fuels such as oil and coal causes global warming. Exxon has since withdrawn this funding.

It is not only the business world that uses PR. In the United States, 3 million supporters of the National Rifle Association (NRA) fund a $100-million-a-year PR campaign against controlling gun ownership. Yet in the United States, the murder rate using guns is many times higher than in countries where guns are controlled.

The NRA has spent millions of members' dollars over the years to convince people that there is no connection between wide ownership of guns and high levels of deaths by shooting. However, many people, like these protestors, are not convinced.

Case Study: Tobacco

In the 1950s, health experts warned that smoking causes diseases—in particular lung cancer. The tobacco industry hired PR firms to challenge this and, with their help, set up the Council for Tobacco Research, headed by a scientist. But, in 1993, it was claimed in court that the work of the council was actually "part of an industry-wide strategy to mislead and confuse the public." By the 1960s, the tobacco industry was paying as much as $20 million a year to argue its case. Later, it spent millions campaigning to make people doubt the dangers of breathing in other people's smoke (secondhand smoke). Despite their campaign, smoking in public places has now been banned in many U.S. states and other countries.

Over the years, tobacco companies spent millions of dollars on promoting smoking as a normal, healthy activity.

• Up for Discussion •

Can you think of any media campaigns that use PR, such as surveys and research, to convince you of something? Do they work, in your opinion?

Disaster!

When charities campaign for money after a disaster, they find the amount of media coverage the disaster receives makes a big difference. The support they get from the media depends partly on how serious the disaster is—but also on where it happens and who is affected.

Case Study: Familiar Places

In December 2004, a massive tsunami struck the Indian Ocean coast, killing as many as 300,000 people, including European and American tourists. Media campaigns in the tourists' countries gave this event major coverage. Newspapers, television, and the Internet publicized numerous appeals that helped to raise funds for aid. The same media gave far less attention to the earthquake that, the following year, devastated the remote Kashmir region of India and Pakistan where few westerners were involved. As a result, much less money was collected for the victims of the earthquake.

The earthquake in Kashmir killed 87,000 people and displaced up to 3 million.

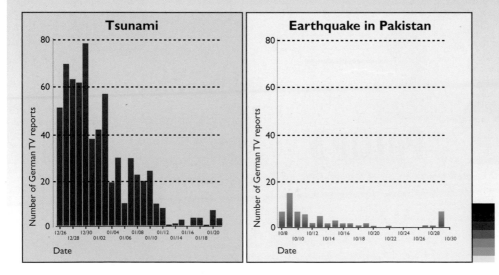

These graphs show the number of German TV reports covering two huge disasters. German donations to Tsunami relief totaled $178 million, while donations to earthquake victims in Pakistan totaled only $8 million.

Millions of people have died and many more have lost their homes in the civil war in the Democratic Republic of Congo. The lack of media coverage can mean a lack of support for people in need.

The Wrong People?

During other disasters, such as war and famine, the interest the media takes can depend on more than how many people are involved and how much they are suffering. For example, the British media is usually more interested in Zimbabwe, which has a historical connection with Britain, than in the neighboring, French-speaking Democratic Republic of Congo (DRC).

The civil war in the DRC had a brief period in the media spotlight in late 2008, but reports were soon overtaken by other news. Media attention can greatly affect the amount of political support and aid a country and its people receive during times of crisis.

The UK's minister for Africa at the time, Lord Malloch-Brown, noticed that "Political will goes . . . up and down depending on the level of public and media concern."

• Up for Discussion •

Will people always be more interested in people and places that they know or can identify with? Why?

"Charity begins at home." What do you think this means? Do you agree?

Raising
the Roof

Sometimes, campaigners try to get maximum media attention for their cause by organizing big public events such as demonstrations, meetings, or concerts.

Case Study: Live Aid

The Live Aid campaign in 1985 was one of the biggest media events of its kind. It was organized by the Irish musician and anti-poverty campaigner Bob Geldof to raise funds for famine relief in Ethiopia. The two main concerts—one in New York and one in London —were televised. Other smaller events took place around the world. Rock stars from around the world took part. More than $140 million was raised.

For campaigning organizations, high-profile events such as Live Aid help to make fundraising easier by increasing public awareness. However, there is a risk that once the event is over, the media and the public may forget about the issues it raised.

The Live Aid concerts in 1985 brought the situation in Ethiopia, where millions were starving, to public notice and raised millions of dollars.

Case Study: Live 8

Twenty years later, in 2005, Bob Geldof organized the Live 8 concerts. These took place simultaneously in each of the wealthy G8 nations, including the U.S., Britain, Japan, and Germany. A concert was also held in South Africa. These were part of a campaign to put pressure on world leaders to "make poverty history" by giving more international aid, canceling countries' debts, and finding a fairer way of organizing world trade. Once again, celebrity musicians took part, performing to an audience of millions of people worldwide. Although the concerts could not, of course, succeed in ending world poverty, they did make the issues surrounding it better understood.

Global superstars such as Madonna performed in the 2005 Live 8 concerts.

Follow-Up

Other high-profile events include Nelson Mandela's 46664 campaign, named after the prison number he received when he was jailed for fighting for freedom in South Africa. This campaign aims to raise awareness about HIV/AIDS. Between 2003 and 2008, the campaign organized concerts in South Africa and other countries. Artists from all over the world took part. Comedians have also banded together in several countries in local Comic Relief campaigns to raise money for a range of causes.

• Up for Discussion •

Do headline-grabbing events make it difficult for less-known campaigns to compete?

What are the implications if a cause becomes fashionable for a while, but then stops getting media coverage?

The Right Face

Campaigners know that the media likes to report on a cause in terms of individual people. This can give the issue a personal touch, which helps people to remember it.

The Right Person

A charity for homeless people will tell one family's story, while an organization raising funds for cancer research may show pictures of a patient who has recovered. The coverage is personal, but it aims to make a general point and raise money for the many other people who need support.

Famous Faces

Another way of linking a cause to a person is by seeking celebrity endorsement. This is when a well-known person takes up a campaign and the media reports on it. The late Princess Diana was a famous example of this. The media loved her and gave massive coverage to her support of the campaign to ban the use of land mines. Her involvement played an important part in getting the cause noticed and in its eventual, partial success.

Images such as this are used by charities to get the public to see people who struggle with problems, such as poverty, as individuals and real people.

Case Study: Figureheads

All over the world, there are political regimes that deny groups of people the right to speak or act freely. Often, campaigns against these regimes concentrate on the plight of an individual and use that person as a case study for the media. The media uses case studies to give a campaign a personal touch that ordinary people can connect with. The human rights organization, Amnesty, has a long history of working this way—but other groups do the same.

For example, Aung San Suu Kyi, the democratically elected leader of Myanmar (Burma) is the world media's "face" of her country's fight for democracy. She had been held under house arrest (not allowed to leave her home) by the military government for most of the time since 1989. In 2009, she was put on trial for breaching the terms of her house arrest. In many ways, Suu Kyi is identified with the struggle for freedom in her country.

• Up for Discussion •

Is there a danger that the public will only be interested in a campaign if we like the person used as a "face" for it? If so, why?

Aung San Suu Kyi has led the opposition against Myanmar's military government since her election in 1990.

A Voice for the Voiceless

Throughout history, campaigners have used the media to speak for people who cannot speak for themselves. These include the very poor, the sick, children, and slaves.

Case Study: Freedom for All

In the 1700s, antislavery campaigners used the media to build sympathy for their cause. They published books and pamphlets, often with firsthand accounts from slaves.

In the United States, a runaway slave, Harriet Tubman, became famous for helping others escape from the plantations of the South and for speaking out against slavery. Harriet Beecher Stowe's novel, Uncle Tom's Cabin (1852), also played a vital role in raising public awareness of slavery.

Harriet Tubman was born a slave in Maryland around 1820. Sarah Bradford helped Harriet Tubman write her autobiography, *Harriet Tubman, the Moses of Her People*, in 1869.

Helping Children Past . . .

As recently as the nineteenth century, it was commonly accepted that adults could treat children as they chose. This included making them work long, grueling hours. Campaigners used the media to draw attention to and challenge this—such as when author Charles Dickens described a child's life in a workhouse in *Oliver Twist* (1838) and in a factory in *David Copperfield* (1849–50).

An example of an early newspaper campaign for children was published in

1885. London journalist W.T. Stead used the paper he edited, the *Pall Mall Gazette,* to highlight the issue of child prostitution with a series of articles in which he described how he had "bought" a 13-year-old girl. The story was a media sensation and landed Stead in prison, but it did eventually help to bring about better child protection laws.

...and Present

In 2004, the International Labor Organization (ILO) estimated that approximately 218 million children worked in factories in poorer parts of the world. Campaigners have used the media to draw public attention to companies that directly or indirectly use child labor—hoping to shame them into stopping. For example, in 2007, a British newspaper, the *Observer*, discovered that Indian child labor was involved in making clothes for suppliers to the Gap fashion chain. As a result, the Indian authorities were alerted and Gap took the clothes off the shelves.

• Up for Discussion •

Occasionally, parts of the media attack campaigners against child labor. They say the issue is complicated and that poor families need the money their children earn. How would you answer this?

Organizations such as UNICEF and the International Labor Organization have used the media to draw world attention to the issue of child labor.

Two Sides to the Story

Campaigners who oppose each other often carry out their arguments through the media by using newspapers and television ads to convey dramatic imagery and language. This can be especially true when it comes to advances in science.

Science in the Media

Explaining science in the media can be difficult for campaigners. Both sides use experts who can help the public to understand the facts and combat common myths and misunderstandings.

The Stem Cell Debate

Medical researchers are looking into ways of using stem cells taken from human embryos that have been created in a laboratory. These stem cells, they believe, could be used to help treat a wide range of conditions including some forms of cancer and Parkinson's disease. Some evangelical Christian groups and the Catholic Church have opposed this technology, which they see as abortion and even murder. Parts of the media have supported this view. However, experts in the field argue that stem cell technology is both acceptable and medically valuable.

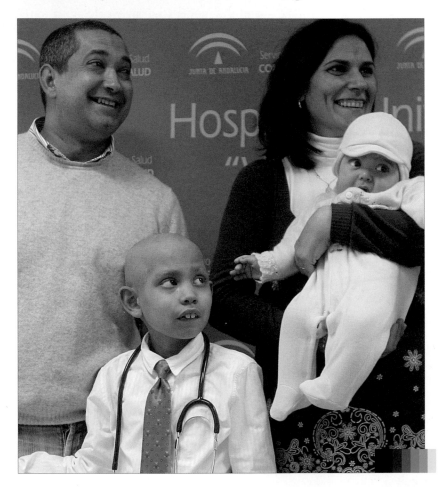

Stem cells taken from his baby brother, Javier, have helped cure seven-year-old Andres (left) of a rare genetic disorder.

An activist opposed to genetically modified crops tears up plants at a test crop site.

The subject of genetically modified (GM) crops needs careful media explanation. These crops have been altered by science, in a way that could not occur naturally, to raise yields or resist drought, pests, or disease. Companies that make GM crops use PR to convince the public that the crops are useful, safe, and can give additional nutritional benefits, as with Golden Rice, a strain of rice that has been bred to include more vitamin A.

However, many people are still suspicious. They use the media to argue that GM crops can damage the environment by crossbreeding with wild plants. They also state that GM crops could damage the economies of poorer farming regions of the world. They accuse GM supporters of over-emphasizing the usefulness of the crops and overlooking the possible dangers.

• Up for Discussion •

Choose a scientific issue and study the way the media covers campaigns around it. How can the media get the facts across clearly?

Conflicting
Causes

The media often has to report on conflicting sets of values when the public is strongly divided about whether a cause is morally or politically right.

A Question of Values

Animal rights campaigners use the media to show pictures of farm animals being raised in confinement to attract public sympathy—but the producers argue that people want cheap meat. People also campaign through their local media against wind farms spoiling their landscape—while environmentalists believe this is a price we have to pay to help end global warming.

Wind farms, such as this one in California, provide clean, renewable energy, but many dislike its impact on the landscape.

A group of Muslim women and children demonstrate in Paris for the right to wear hijabs in state public schools.

Few issues are as hotly debated as the hijab (head covering) that many Muslim women wear. In France, the argument reached a peak in 2004 when the government banned "religious symbols" from being worn in public schools. This included Christian crosses and Jewish skullcaps, as well as hijabs. The government, and its supporters in the media, stressed that the ban reflected the French tradition of keeping religion out of education, and, therefore, it was not favoring any one faith over another.

Many people, including some Muslims, believed that the government was right. But because the media paid most attention to the hijab, some Muslims accused the government of running a campaign directed against the Islamic faith.

Antiracist and human rights campaigners joined in. The U.S.-based organization Human Rights Watch said the ban "would violate the rights to freedom of religion and expression." The French newspaper Le Monde wrote that passing the law would lead to "marginalizing and excluding a part of the population" (December 2003).

To antiracist campaigners, it appeared that the media whipped up feelings specifically against Muslims.

• Up for Discussion •

Would media coverage of the hijab debate be different in Muslim and non-Muslim countries? How might it differ?

Slow Burn

Sometimes it takes years for the media to take an interest in a campaign. Fights to right past injustices often fall into this category. Often, the first step is to convince the media—and the public—that a wrong has been done in the first place.

Out of Sight . . .

In 1974, 21 people died in two bomb attacks in Birmingham, England. Six men were found guilty of carrying out the bombing on behalf of the IRA (Irish Republican Army), which was fighting the British in Northern Ireland. The men were innocent—but it took a long time to convince the media and public of this. Campaigns in their support did not really take off for 10 years until TV programs had been made about the case and Chris Mullin, member of Parliament and author, published *Error of Judgement* (1986). The men were freed in 1991.

Members of the Birmingham Six were freed in 1991 after 17 years of appeals and campaigning.

Case Study: The Stolen Generations, Australia

From about 1910 to 1970 in Australia, approximately 100,000 mixed-race Aboriginal children were taken from their parents. Most were raised in children's homes. Many white Australians saw this as "rescuing" them from Aboriginal life.

In 1981, historian Peter Read published The Stolen Generations, a report that showed the harm that had been done to the children and their families.

Read's opinion was supported by a national inquiry. In 2001, the story was brought to the world by a film, Rabbit Proof Fence, that told it through the eyes of two children. Most Australians now supported a formal apology to the Aboriginal people on behalf of the Australian government—but not all.

As late as 2004, journalist Andrew Bolt still argued in Australia's Sunday Mail that there was no evidence of "stolen" children—only abandoned ones. The apology came at last, in 2008, from Australian Prime Minister Kevin Rudd.

• Up for Discussion •

Why do you think that the media take a long time to support some campaigns or may never do so?

A scene from the 2001 film, Rabbit Proof Fence, helped to put pressure on the Australian government for an apology to the Stolen Generations.

Straight Talk

The media can play an important part in government campaigns to educate the public. These include encouraging healthy eating and exercising. These companies also make people aware of the dangers and illegality, in most countries, of drinking alcohol and then driving.

Effective Measures

Media campaigns against drinking and driving can be very effective. For example, TV, newspapers, and magazines may show pictures of people who were killed or badly injured by drunk drivers. The June 2004 issue of the *American Journal of Preventive Medicine* suggested that these images can reduce alcohol-related car crashes by up to 13 percent. Media campaigns have also encouraged drivers to wear a seatbelt and to observe the speed limit.

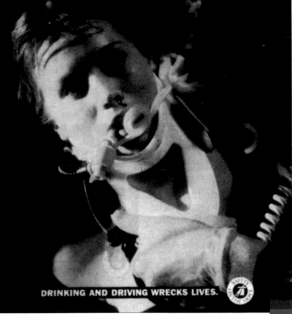

Because many countries have used the media to educate people about the dangers of drinking and driving, many lives have been saved.

• Up for Discussion •

What educational campaigns do you think are especially important for people in your age group?

Case Study: HIV/AIDS in Africa

HIV, the virus that causes AIDS, spreads mainly through sex. In sub-Saharan Africa, the disease took hold long before it was identified. An estimated 22 million people are now infected. There is no cure, and treatment is very expensive. Education about prevention is especially important. This can be difficult because, in many countries, there is a tradition of not talking about sex. There are also widespread misconceptions about how the illness is contracted.

The Ugandan government has risen to the challenge with a major media campaign using newspapers, billboards, and radio. This has helped to bring infection rates down from an estimated 20 percent to about 6 percent. The Straight Talk organization has taken on the important job of communicating with young people. Straight Talk began in 1993 as a newspaper for 10–19-year-olds and now also offers information and counseling, produces informative radio programs, publishes a magazine for primary schoolchildren, and has an Internet presence.

In South Africa, where infection rates among adults are approximately 18 percent, HIV has been introduced into popular TV soap operas. Other countries, including Cambodia and India, also use soap operas to spread the word about HIV. In a survey in India, more than 70 percent of people said they had received their information about HIV and AIDS from television. Popular media coverage such as this can save lives.

A sign in Zambia, Africa, reminds people that children become victims too when their parents die of AIDS.

The Media as Campaigner

Sometimes, the media becomes a campaigner in its own right. However, it may not always give the whole picture.

Getting it Wrong?

"Megan's law" in the United States is named after a child murdered in 1994 by a sex offender. The law states that information about where known child abusers live must be made public. In Britain, the News of the World has campaigned for a similar law. But opponents believe that this encourages dangerous people to go into hiding, away from police supervision. They add that such laws overlook the fact that most abuse is carried out by people who the children already know.

The family of Megan Kanka watched the New Jersey governor sign a bill that created an Internet register of sex offenders in the state.

Case Study: The MMR Myth

In the early 2000s, there was a major media panic in Britian. It involved newspapers, radio, television, and the Internet. It was about the vaccination routinely given to children to prevent measles, mumps, and rubella (MMR). It followed an article in a medical journal that suggested the vaccination could trigger autism. Almost no experts agreed. The Guardian's specialist science writer, Ben Goldacre, called it "a hoax." But parents were scared, vaccination levels dropped, and there was a dangerous increase in disease.

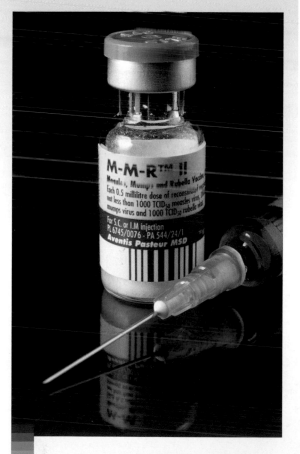

The controversial MMR vaccine

Getting it Right

Media campaigns can have positive results. In the 1950s and early 1960s, the drug thalidomide was given to pregnant women suffering from morning sickness. It was withdrawn in 1962, because it caused babies to be born with missing limbs and other health problems. In 1972, the *Sunday Times* campaigned to make thalidomide's British distributors pay high levels of compensation to affected families. The paper went on to show that thalidomide had not been tested properly, and claims were made against its manufacturer.

Campaigns elsewhere had less success. Victims in Germany received less than half the average amount of compensation paid in Britain. In Italy, Spain, and Austria, victims received nothing.

• *Up for Discussion* •

What other media-led campaigns can you think of?

Which of these do you think were useful—and which less so? Why?

29

Making News

Campaigners can get media coverage for their causes by doing something dramatic to be noticed. This can include carrying out daring stunts and breaking the law.

Fighting Fathers

Fathers 4 Justice is a group that campaigns for better access to children for divorced or separated fathers. It began in Britain and now extends internationally. It is famous for stunts, which have included climbing the London Eye and scaling Buckingham Palace. Critics say the stunts do the cause more harm than good. But there is no doubt they get media attention.

Green Campaigners

The environmental campaigning organization Greenpeace has a history of making dramatic gestures. In recent years, it has drawn attention to the damaging effects of greenhouse gases, which most scientists believe are causing Earth's climate to change and become warmer. Greenpeace members have blockaded coal-burning power stations. In 2008, they dumped coal outside a hotel in Warsaw, the capital of Poland, during an important international meeting about the future of coal. They also floated a huge balloon over a coal-fired power station in Australia, with the slogan "No future in coal."

ACCESS DENIED. DON'T LET LABOUR STOP YOU BEING A SUPERDAD. FATHERS 4 JUSTICE

Three members of Fathers 4 Justice, dressed as superheroes Captain America, Robin, and Batman, protest on a ledge outside the UK Foreign Office.

Greenpeace members draw attention to climate change by building a replica of Noah's Ark on the slopes of Mount Ararat, where tradition says the Ark ended its journey.

• Up for Discussion •

Why is a stunt, which may break the law and even be dangerous, a good way to get media attention?

Can stunts result in bad media coverage? Can this harm a cause or campaign?

Case Study:
An Inconvenient Truth

In 2006, former U.S. Vice President Al Gore was so concerned by U.S. attitudes toward climate change that he made a film about it called An Inconvenient Truth. At the time, the U.S. government was sympathetic to the minority of scientists who doubted that climate change really is the result of human activity. The U.S. media gave airtime and space to these doubters, claiming that they were being balanced and leading the public to believe that the causes of climate change really are open to question. Gore's film, along with a web site and meetings addressed by Gore, aimed to challenge the doubters—and to get people to act.

Scare Tactics

"It [Chernobyl] was the worst nuclear accident ... ever seen ... The fallout, 400 times more radioactivity than ... at Hiroshima, drove a third of a million people from their homes and triggered an epidemic of thyroid cancer ...." (*National Geographic*, April 2006).

Case Study: Nuclear Fear

In April 1986, the explosion at the Chernobyl nuclear plant in Ukraine, was the industry's worst nightmare. But campaigners had long warned of the dangers of nuclear power. A film called The China Syndrome *(1979) dramatized the possibility of an accident only months before a real-life, near disaster at the Three Mile Island nuclear plant in Pennsylvania.*

No one knows how many deaths Chernobyl has caused over the years from the effects of radiation. One Greenpeace estimate was 90,000. Other estimates ran into millions.

Public fears make it easy for antinuclear campaigners to get coverage for other concerns, such as the problem of radiation leaks and the difficulty of storing highly dangerous nuclear waste safely. In many countries, such campaigns have had a certain amount of success. In Sweden, safety issues have led the authorities to decide—at least for now—to phase out nuclear power.

A reactor at the Chernobyl nuclear power station exploded on April 26, 1986, releasing dangerous radioactive material into the atmosphere.

AIDS

HOW BIG DOES IT HAVE TO GET BEFORE YOU TAKE NOTICE?

[GAY OR STRAIGHT, MALE OR FEMALE, ANYONE CAN GET AIDS FROM SEXUAL INTERCOURSE. SO THE MORE PARTNERS, THE GREATER THE RISK. PROTECT YOURSELF, USE A CONDOM.]

Crying Wolf?

In the early 1980s, the world first learned about AIDS. Governments in many countries responded with major campaigns, warning the population of an epidemic that could, in the words of a British television advertisement, "kill through ignorance." Scare stories about AIDS still circulate with lurid tales of people "deliberately" infecting others.

But how effective are scare stories? The massive AIDS epidemic in western Europe and the United States has still not occurred—although it has in Africa. Similarly, supporters of nuclear power say that its dangers have been exaggerated. If messages seem to be overplayed, is there a danger that people will start to ignore them— or doubt them altogether?

This 1986 television advertisement aimed to change people's behavior as a response to AIDS. Some critics think the advertisements did more harm than good as people stopped reacting to scare tactics.

• Up for Discussion •

How can we judge whether things are as bad as the media—or a campaign that uses the media—says they are?

Giving the People What They Want?

Media outlets tend to have an idea about who their audience is and what they will be interested in. This can affect the way they report —or do not report—on a whole range of issues.

Case Study: War and Antiwar

There has been much criticism of the war in Iraq, but antiwar campaigners complain that it can be difficult to get their views heard in the media.

The war against Afghanistan began in 2001, after terrorists attacked New York and Washington, D.C., on September 11. The U.S. government believed that Osama bin Laden, the leader of the group, al Qaeda, that was responsible for the attacks, was being sheltered in Afghanistan.

Two years later, the United States and other countries, including Britain, attacked Iraq. They said Iraq had weapons of mass destruction. This was later found to be untrue. Some U.S. government officials wrongly claimed there were links between the government of Iraq and al Qaeda—a view reported by, among others, the television network Fox News.

Demonstrations against the war in Iraq occurred all over the world and were widely reported in the media. However, once the war was underway, the antiwar movement claimed that it became more difficult to get media attention. One explanation may be that many media outlets believe the public wants to support soldiers in Iraq in their mission. Therefore, they may choose not to include stories or reports that appear to criticize it.

Fear of Terrorism

Since the 9/11 attacks, a fear of terrorism has encouraged governments to pass laws restricting people's freedoms. In the United States and Britain, suspected terrorists have been deported or imprisoned for periods of time without trials. Campaigners for human rights find it difficult to get the media to support challenges to this. The media goes along with—even supports—what it feels is public opinion.

• Up for Discussion •

Should the media take any notice of public or government opinion? Why?

Is it possible for the media to cover a controversial campaign and not take sides about it? How?

In the aftermath of 9/11, many al Qaeda suspects were held by the U.S. military at Guantanamo Bay Naval Base in Cuba.

A Bad Light

Sometimes, the media seems to join in with campaigns of hostility toward certain groups of people—and anyone who dares to speak up for them.

Immigration

Immigrants, especially those who arrive as refugees, are often faced with media hostility. Australia's Refugee Council, for example, reports that "Refugees, asylum seekers and the Australians who support them have had to endure countless media articles full of inaccuracies ... sometimes media organizations ... publish information which is blatantly false."

In Britain, some newspapers behave in a similar way, such as the *Daily Express* articles titled "Asylum seekers use your taxes to smuggle in relatives" and "Asylum seekers get free holidays." Such coverage can make it difficult for the public to get a fair picture. However, when groups of people are persecuted or treated badly, supportive pressure groups do exist.

Immigrant Mexicans work in California. Immigrants often suffer prejudice from local people who are afraid that the newcomers will take their jobs. This attitude is often encouraged by the media.

A Roma settlement in Italy. The Roma often experience discrimination in housing, employment, and education. Many live in poverty.

In the 700 years since the Roma ethnic group (once called Gypsies) arrived in Europe from India, they have been romanticized in songs and stories. They also have been accused of being thieves, pickpockets, kidnappers, and murderers. During World War II, approximately 600,000 Roma were killed in concentration camps. It is a reflection of the media attitude toward the Roma that this tragedy is often forgotten today.

Media coverage of Roma issues continues this tradition. For example, in Italy in 2007, the media did little to challenge politicians who suggested that the Roma—including Italian Roma—should be deported, even after Roma homes were attacked.

Elsewhere in Europe, where the Roma usually live in the poorest housing with high levels of unemployment, little effort is made by the media to challenge the racism the Roma suffer. In fact, the media often makes it worse.

For example, in 1991, in the Polish town of Mawa, a local radio station accused a young Roma man of running away after a fatal car accident. Local papers repeated this and a group of townspeople attacked the local Roma community for five days.

• Up for Discussion •

What examples can you find of popular campaigns against groups of people? What part does the media play in these campaigns?

Make the Media
Work for You

Campaigning can be hard work and takes time. But it is now possible for people—even those with few resources—to launch their own campaigns.

Internet Campaigning

With user-generated video sites, such as YouTube, it is possible for campaigners to produce their films and share them with thousands of people. Social networking sites such as Facebook and Twitter can also be used. E-mail can be used to inform supporters about what a campaign is doing and guide them to web sites and blogs that feature news. They can also keep in touch using text messages.

The Avaaz organization, for example, updates millions of supporters all over the world by e-mail, giving news about its campaign "to close the gap between the world we have, and the world most people everywhere want." The U.S.-based group Moveon.org came to prominence during the Internet antiwar campaign. It has branched out into a range of campaigns on other issues, including reform of the media. The Internet can be a powerful tool for campaigning. However, it is often best to use a combination of different media to draw attention to issues and to follow up on them.

Handwritten messages to President Obama fill a wall erected by the Avaaz group in Washington, D.C.

Case Study: Find Madeleine

An example of a campaign that has been widely reported in the news media, but which also makes good use of the Internet, is the search for Madeleine McCann.

Four-year-old Madeleine vanished from a resort apartment in Portugal in May 2007. The story of her parents' search for her remained in the news for months.

The media coverage was not always sympathetic and sometimes inaccurate, but it did mean that it was almost impossible for anyone not to know about Madeleine. Since her disappearance, Madeleine's parents have used the Internet to raise funds to help in the search for their missing daughter and to publish news about it and pictures of Madeleine. They have worked to keep the story in the news in the hope that they will one day learn the truth about what happened to their little girl.

When four-year-old Madeleine McCann was abducted from a resort apartment in Portugal, her parents launched a worldwide media campaign to find her.

• Up for Discussion •

Learn about campaigns run by young people. How have they used the media and created their own media coverage using the Internet?

Glossary

aboriginal The earliest inhabitants of a region, such as the people who lived in Australia before the first settlers from Europe arrived.

AIDS Acquired Immune Deficiency Syndrome. It is a disease that destroys a person's ability to fight infections.

animal rights Opposition to using animals for research, treating them cruelly, and killing them for their furs.

campaign Organized activities aimed at making a change in the way governments, or people in general, behave.

cause A movement that people support and campaign for.

civil war War between two or more groups of people in a single country.

climate change A shift in the world's climate.

compensation A payment or other award given to someone who has suffered a loss or injury.

demonstration A march or large meeting held to draw attention to an issue.

deport To expel someone from a country.

embryo A human in its early stages of development before it is born.

epidemic A widespread infectious disease.

global warming The gradual warming of Earth's climate.

GM crops Crops that have been altered by scientists to contain genes that would not occur in the crop naturally.

hijab A special kind of head covering worn by some Muslim women.

human rights Our rights as human beings. The United Nations has published a Universal Declaration of Human Rights that lists these rights.

immigrant A person who moves into a foreign country or region to live.

international aid Funds given by one country to another for help in times of difficulty.

media The methods we use to communicate. These include newspapers, radio, television, film, magazines, books, and the Internet.

nuclear reactor The part of a nuclear power station where atoms are split to make the energy used in the power station.

persecute To mistreat a person or group of people, often because of their race or religion.

press release A written communication to the media to inform them about an event that has happened or is about to happen.

pressure group A group that tries to influence public opinion and policy making, in particular, government policy making.

public relations The job of communicating the work of an organization to the media.

radiation Energy in the form of particles or electromagnetic waves. In larger doses, radiation can be harmful to humans.

radioactivity The energy created when atoms are broken or split.

refugee Someone who flees from their home or country, often because of war.

Roma The proper name for the people once called Gypsies. They are descended from a group of people who left India between the eleventh and fifteenth centuries and settled in much of Europe. Traditionally, they were nomads, but many are now settled.

rubella A disease caused by a virus. It is often called German measles. If a pregnant woman has the disease, it can harm her unborn child.

stem cell A body cell that can develop into any other kind of body cell.

terrorism Carrying out violent attacks for political reasons.

tsunami A huge wave in the ocean that can form after an earthquake.

vaccination Infecting someone with a very mild form of a germ that causes disease so the person's body is able to fight off the germs in future. It is also called immunization.

wind farm A group of wind turbines (motors with large blades that turn in the wind). Turbines are used to generate electricity using energy from the wind.

Further Information

Books

Anderson, Judith. Working for Our Future series. Sea-to-Sea Publications, 2010.

Botzakis, Stergios. What's Your Source?: Questioning the News. (Media Literacy) Capstone Press, 2009.

Connolly, Sean. Getting the Message series. Smart Apple Media, 2010.

Hibbert, Adam. The Power of the Media. (What's Your View?) Smart Apple Media, 2007.

Kramer, Ann. Human Rights: Who Decides? (Behind the News) Heinemann Library, 2007.

Web Sites

http://www.unicef.org/righttoknow/index_mediacampaign.html
This site gives advice from the UN Children's organization on how to start a media campaign.

www.ilo.org/ipec/lang--en/index.htm
International Programme on the Elimination of Child Labour (IPEC) works toward eliminating child labor. Young people speak out against child labor.

http://www.pbs.org/wnet/wideangle/episodes/young-muslim-and-french/headscarf-headlines-around-the-world/france/2617/
This site discusses the issue of the Muslim hijab.

http://www.unionromani.org/pueblo_in.htm
This site provides a brief history and the social issues the Roma people face today.

www.broadcasthivafrica.org
This site provides information about and protection from HIV/AIDS across Africa.

http://www.marchofdimes.com/professionals/14332_1172.asp#head1
This site explains the history of thalidomide and how it may help HIV/AIDS patients.

http://www.climatecrisis.net/takeaction/
Learn about Al Gore's film An Inconvenient Truth and how you can become active in the fight against global warming.

http://reconciliaction.org.au/nsw/education-kit/stolen-generations/
Read about the Stolen Generation.

http://www.fair.org/index.php?page=100
FAIR is a media watch dog that works with activists and journalists.

http://www.journalismethics.ca/ethics_in_news/bass.htm
This site discusses ethics in journalism.

http://pol.moveon.org
Citizens unite on various issues that are often dominated by backers with money and the media.

Note to parents and teachers: Every effort has been made by the publishers to ensure that these web sites are suitable for children, are of the highest educational value, and contain no inappropriate or offensive material. However, because of the nature of the Internet, it is impossible to guarantee that the contents of these sites will not be altered. We strongly advise that Internet access be supervised by a responsible adult.

Index

Numbers in **bold** refer to captions for illustrations.

Explore the other titles in the *Media Power* series.

MAR   2011